Feast of the Seven Fishes

An Italian Christmas and More with Divine Delectables by Deborah

Deborah Lugo DeMatteis

ISBN-10: 1502498189
ISBN-13: 978-1502498182

To my mother and father - my love for you will live forever and you will always be in my heart.

CONTENTS

ACKNOWLEDGMENTS

I would like to express my gratefulness to so many people who supported me through this book, to all of those, past and present, who granted me the opportunity to learn from them, and perfect my cooking skills, to those who allowed me to quote their remarks and assisted in the editing, proofreading and design.

I would like to thank my father, who was my first cooking influence. He taught me that cooking took time and patience to perfect the end result. He taught me the importance of family, the act of love, kindness and that caring for those you love was the only path to take with family.

I would like to thank my aunts, Angie, Josie, Dotty, Fanny and Jean, for their influence in my life with sharing their recipes, their cooking skills and talent, along with the long history of our family's Italian traditions. More importantly, including my mother, I thank each of them for never deviating from conveying the message, showing or displaying the behaviors that taught us the importance of the family bond.

Thank you to my mother-in-law, Angela, who taught me how presentation, taste, and perfection, along with a love and passion for food and cooking were all essentials in the kitchen. The greatest lesson I learned from her was the true gift of self-gratification you receive in return, from having the people you love, always walk away from your table completely satisfied.

Thank you to my family, Michele, Jeannette, Gabe, Jennifer, Nicholas, Meredith, Michael, Monica, Julianna, Adamo, Olivia, Ava, Vincent, Mateo, Antonio and William, without our commitment to our family heritage and traditions, this book would never have been written.

A special thank you to my longtime friend, Susan. You have been a true friend to me for many years, and I am forever grateful for your friendship, your kind and caring heart, and your unconditional love and support. You are a rare individual, friend, and you have taught me to see the laughter in most things. Thank you for your talent and support with the photographs, editing, proofreading and for sharing your marketing expertise.

Last but not least, I thank all of those who have supported me and who have been in my corner over the years, from my cousins to close friends to my extended family. Please forgive me for not mentioning each of you by name. There are just too many of you, but I believe you know who you are.

THE CHRISTMAS STORY

Christmas is such a magical time of year, and to the Italians, *La Vigilia di Natale* (Christmas Eve) is considered the most magical, and joyful night of the year. Italians share a rich culture, a love of food, along with strong religious, and family values. Holiday meals have always been an essential part of my multi-cultural heritage, and while every culture has its own traditions, I am not sure any other culture celebrates any tradition with more passion than the Italians. As far back as I can remember, and till this day, Christmas Eve has always been a special time for family and friends to gather together to celebrate, reminisce about the past, create memories, and share a delicious meal.

Growing up in a Hispanic and Italian-American household, it was the Italian-American culture that dominated our celebration with the traditional Italian Christmas Eve dinner, always to be known as the *Feast of the Seven Fishes, (Festa dei Sette Pesci)*. This feast is a meal without meat honoring the midnight birth of baby Jesus. It is by far, my favorite holiday of all, and if you come from an Italian family, you are more than likely familiar with the tradition, and its history. If not, allow me to take you on a small journey of its rich Italian history.

The exact origin of this tradition is somewhat debatable, however, history states it's a custom that originated in Southern Italy, which spread throughout Italy, and around the world. Others believe it originated with the first Italian immigrants to the New World as a way to celebrate the bounty of the New World. Italians and Italian-Americans alike still celebrate this old-world custom that has been handed down from generation to generation, and in my home, it's an Italian traditional feast to be remembered, and cherished for many years to come. Just ask anyone that has sat at my Christmas Eve table.

Some may ask why seven fishes? There are several religious philosophies that support the early stages of this symbolic feast, but the most common belief is that the seven fishes represent the seven sacraments of the Roman Catholic Church. However, some Italian families have been known to celebrate with not only seven fishes but twelve, and even thirteen different types of seafood dishes. While seven may represent the number of the Catholic sacraments, twelve is believed to represent the number of Apostles, and together with Jesus, made a table of thirteen, at the last supper. Whatever the number may be, the meal is believed to bring *buona fortuna* (good fortune) in the New Year.

There are no rules as to which types of fish are served. However, some of the most popular that have been known to be eaten on this special holiday are prepared variations of calamari, baccalà (salted cod fish), oysters, scallops, eel, clams, and shrimp. The feast always begins with antipasto, and on a typical Napolitano table, this could include broccoli rabe, anchovies, spaghetti with garlic and oil, clams, fried eel, cheeses, eggplant caponata, followed by other fish dishes. The dinner portion of the meal is typically wrapped up with a *caponate di pesce* (fish salad). The meal always ended with dessert, which included many mouthwatering, and different types of traditional dolci, such as Panettone, Struffoli, Zeppole, along with assorted fruit, and nuts. After the meal, many Italians attend the traditional Christmas Eve midnight mass. Some also may simply uncover the small baby Jesus figurine in the manger of their **Presepe** (Nativity scene), in their home, and pray. After midnight, many would celebrate the birth of Jesus with sparkling, and bubbly Spumante or Prosecco, and then open the presents, the moment every child anxiously waited for.

My childhood memories of Christmas Eve were always spent at my Aunt Fanny's. I have such fond memories of those Christmas Eve's spent in her home, and this is where it all began for me with learning how to cook the most treasured Christmas Eve traditional seafood dishes. She was a phenomenal cook, who spent days prepping, and preparing the feast. Everything that emerged from her stove or oven to the dining room table were wonderful dishes, and absolutely delicious. Her Christmas Eve table was always filled with seafood dishes such as, clams on the half shell, fried shrimp, shrimp cocktail, baccalà, fried flounder, stuffed calamari, and a sauce filled with all types of fish, from shrimp, mussels and lobster to calamari, which was served over linguine. It was a given that a gallon of Gallo Burgundy wine and a bottle of cream soda would be set between my Uncle John and my Dad, who each Christmas would mix a tall glass of both with ice, and they would share a holiday drink, together.

Their home always felt warm, welcoming, along with being decorated beautifully, and the fireplace always added an extra touch of warmth to their home. Hours, prior to midnight, were spent eating, the adults playing cards while my cousins, my sisters and I played and waited, with much anticipation, for Aunt Fanny's grandfather clock to make that chime sound as it struck the midnight hour. The chime always prompted a celebration of opening presents, and believe it or not, more eating. Magically, my aunt would appear from the kitchen with a tray of Italian delicacies that included cured meats, hams, roasted chicken, and more. The eating began all over again. You never left Aunt Fanny's and Uncle John's house until well after midnight, and it was a given that my sisters and I always fell fast asleep on the ride home, which was only from one side of Mount Vernon to the other.

It is those Italian family traditions that I have learned from, and they are the traditions I continue, today, with the hope of them being passed on for generations to come. In today's economy, the traditional meal has become an expensive meal to put on the table, and some tend to believe it is a lot of work (and it is) but for me, a traditional Italian Christmas Eve meal is a given, no questions asked, and it is an important family gathering, in my home. I will make whatever sacrifices I need to ensure it is nothing less than the standards and expectations that have been instilled in me since I was a young girl.

It takes days, and weeks to prepare for, from decorating, to baking, to cleaning fish, prepping, and preparing, along with cooking it all but with everything that goes into it, I wouldn't change a thing. I have been hosting, and preparing Christmas Eve dinner for as long as I can remember, and it's a holiday where I am in my place of complete peace, joy, creativity, and contentment. There is an excitement that fills my heart, and it brings me a sense of pride, love, and without a doubt, a day of unconditional giving to my family. I don't believe there is one member of my family who doesn't have a great anticipation, and appreciation of my Christmas Eve feast.

While the menu has slightly changed over the years, for the most part, some dishes will just never change, and are an absolute given that they will be on my Christmas Eve table.

The meal begins with antipasto, and some staples are my famous **Onion Focaccia Bread**, and **Pizza Bread**, along with **Broccoli Rabe, Eggplant Caponata, Little Neck Clams** on the half shell, **Shrimp Cocktail, Crab Cakes, Mussels with White Wine and Garlic**, and my famous **Scungilli Salad**, which a dear friend says, *is by far the best he ever had.* A **Baccalà Salad** or a baccalà stew with potatoes in a tomato sauce were always a staple on my table until the passing of both of my parents. It remained on the menu as a symbolic remembrance of their presence for many years but it always wound up being thrown away so I discontinued making it. Christmas Eve was my parent's favorite holiday, and while their presence is sorely missed at my table, it's the fond memories of Christmas Eve's of the past, which bring a sense of peace to my heart, and a smile to my face.

The second course is always *Zuppa di Pesce*, which can vary each year, however, for the most part, includes shrimp, clams, mussels, and calamari, all served over linguine.

The last course is an array of several fish dishes, which can include *Stuffed Calamari*, *Fried Filet of Grey Sole*, *Coconut Shrimp*, and steamed *Alaskan King Crab*. In the last few years, the Alaskan King Crab has been removed, and replaced with *Lobsters*. Lastly, there are my ultimate *Baked Clams*, and rarely are there less than seven dozen on my table. There is typically a contest as to who can eat the most baked clams, and my older sister always wins, with my son coming in as a close second. Ironically, my sister is the smallest of all the women, and we are not quite sure where she puts all the food she consumes.

The meal always ends with dessert, which includes trays of baked Christmas cookies, Struffoli, Zeppoles, Pizzelle (made by daughter-in-law), and always a special surprise dessert that is whipped up by Nana. It can be anything from Mini Chocolate Cheesecakes to Pumpkin Mousse Parfaits to Chocolate Truffle Cups to Mini Lemon Curd Meringue Pies. Whatever it is, it will be a surprise, and most certainly, delicious.

The evening comes to an end, when you finally give in to that relentless question from my grandchild to my great niece and great nephews since they arrived, *"Is it time to open presents?"* Then the chaos, which is overshadowed by laughter and excitement begins. Wrapping paper, Christmas bags, tissue paper, and boxes are flying everywhere. The screams, and gasps of excitement are heard throughout the house. No matter how hard you try, the excitement is something that you can't control and is something that you never want to miss nor one that you will ever forget. While the excitement of presents is important to all of them, there isn't a one of them, if you asked, that couldn't tell you the true meaning of Christmas. It's all about the celebration, the miracle, the blessings, family, and the birth of baby Jesus.

However you celebrate the miracles of the season, I hope each of you are surrounded by the love of your families and friends, and may the spirit of Christmas fill your heart with peace, joy, and hope for the New Year.

Buon Natale e felice anno nuovo!

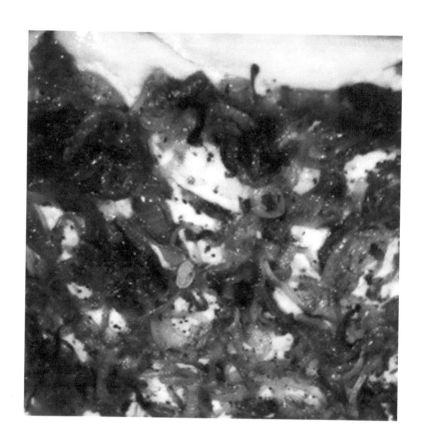

DEBORAH'S ONION FOCACCIA BREAD

Ingredients

1 large pizza dough, homemade or store bought

2 large onions, sliced thin   1 tsp. kosher salt

1/2 tsp. dried oregano   1/2 tsp. coarse black pepper

Extra virgin olive oil   All-purpose flour, for dusting

9 ½ x 2 ¾ round aluminum deep pan

Directions

Preheat oven to 375°F. Dust pizza dough lightly with flour. Drizzle extra virgin olive oil in the bottom of the pan (just enough to coat lightly). Place the dough in the pan and drizzle the top lightly with additional extra virgin olive oil. Cover the dough with a dish towel or plastic wrap. Place the pan in a warm area near the stove and let the dough rise for at least 3 - 4 hours. Overnight is recommended.

Cut the onions in half, lengthwise and slice each half thinly. Heat 2 tbsp. of extra virgin olive oil in a sauté pan. Be careful to not burn the oil. Add the onions, season with salt, pepper and oregano. Slowly sauté the onions until caramelized.

Once the dough has risen, spread the sautéed caramelized onions evenly over the top and poke a few holes in the top of dough for the flavors to run through the focaccia during the baking process.

Place in the oven for 35 to 45 minutes or until golden brown. The focaccia will continue to rise during the baking process. Serve warm or at room temperature. Serve the focaccia with good quality extra virgin olive oil, for dipping, flavored with crushed garlic and crushed red pepper flakes.

SQUILLANTE FAMILY'S PIZZA BREAD

Ingredients

1 large pizza dough, homemade or store bought

32 oz. can whole plum tomatoes (Scalfani® is my preference)

Kosher salt, to taste   Coarse black pepper, to taste

Fresh Basil   Extra virgin olive oil

1/4 cup Parmagiano Reggiano cheese, grated

All-purpose flour, for dusting

9 ½ x 2 ¾ round aluminum deep pan or a lasagna pan (2 pizza dough's are recommended for a lasagna pan size)

Directions

Preheat oven to 375°F. Dust pizza dough lightly with flour. Drizzle extra virgin olive oil in the bottom of pan (just enough to coat lightly). Place the dough in the pan and drizzle the top lightly with additional extra virgin olive oil. Cover the dough with a dish towel or plastic wrap. Place the pan in a warm area near the stove and let the dough rise for at least 3 - 4 hours. Overnight is recommended.

Once the dough has risen, poke a few holes in the top using your fingers. Take one whole plum tomato at a time and gently squeeze it with your hands over the top of the dough. Repeat this step with 5 - 6 more tomatoes. Drizzle very little tomato juice from the can over the top. Do not overdo this step, as the bread will get soggy during the baking process. Sprinkle the top of the bread with the kosher salt, pepper and grated cheese. Decorate the top with the cured Sicilian olives, pushing gently into the dough and with the basil leaves, as shown. Drizzle a little olive oil over the top.

Place in the oven for 35 to 45 minutes or until bottom of the bread is a nice golden brown. Serve warm or at room temperature.

EGGPLANT CAPONATA

Ingredients

6 tbsp. extra virgin olive oil

2 baby eggplant, unpeeled, cut and cubed

1 red bell pepper, diced

1/2 cup calamata olives, chopped

1/2 cup golden raisins

2 tbsp. capers, drained

Kosher salt, to taste

1/2 cup pine nuts, toasted

2 celery stalks, sliced thin

1 large onion, diced

2 garlic cloves, minced

1 (6 oz. can) tomato paste

2 tbsp. balsamic vinegar

1/4 cup fresh basil, chopped

Coarse black pepper, to taste

Directions

Heat oil in heavy large sauté pan over medium heat. Add eggplant, onion, celery, red bell pepper and garlic. Sauté until vegetables are soft and slightly brown, about 15 minutes. Add the tomato paste, balsamic vinegar, raisins, calamata olives and drained capers.

Simmer until tender, stirring occasionally, about 15 minutes. If caponata is too thick, add a little water. Season with salt and pepper, to taste. Add fresh basil and toasted pine nuts, mix gently. Transfer to a serving bowl. Serve warm or at room temperature with good crusty bread.

NANNY ANGIE'S BROCCOLI RABE

Ingredients

1 bunch, broccoli rabe, tough stems removed, cleaned and rough chopped

Extra virgin olive oil

1 large onion, sliced thin

4 garlic cloves, smashed

Red pepper flakes, to taste

Kosher salt, to taste

Directions

Coat the bottom of a large sauté pan with olive oil. Add the onion, garlic and red pepper flakes. Sauté until the onion is soft and lightly caramelized.

Remove tough stems from the broccoli rabe, rough chop and wash, thoroughly. Add the broccoli rabe to pan with the onions and garlic. Lower the heat to medium low and sauté broccoli rabe until wilted and tender, approx. 8 - 10 minutes.

Remove broccoli rabe from pan and place in a serving bowl. Set aside. Let the olive oil, onions, garlic and red pepper flakes cool in the pan. Once cooled, pour over the top of broccoli rabe and serve immediately or at room temperature. Serve with good crusty bread or with focaccia bread.

DEBORAH'S SCUNGILLI SALAD

Ingredients

29 oz. can La Monica Scungilli®, cleaned and large pieces cut in half

2 tbsp. extra virgin olive oil

1 small red onion, sliced thin

1 red bell pepper, roasted and sliced thin

2 stalks celery, sliced thin

1 garlic clove, minced

1/2 cup cured Sicilian olives

1 cup cherry tomatoes, whole or halved

Kosher salt, to taste

Coarse black pepper, to taste

1 lemon, juiced

2 tbsp. flat-leaf parsley, chopped

Directions

Preheat oven to 400°F. In a roasting pan, place the red bell pepper, drizzle lightly with extra virgin olive oil and kosher salt. Roast the pepper until all sides are blackened, approx. 20 - 30 minutes. Remove from the oven and place the pepper in a small bowl and cover with plastic wrap until it is cool enough to handle. Remove the blackened outer skin of the pepper, remove the veins and seeds. Slice the pepper into thin strips and set aside.

Drain and rinse the scungilli well and place in a serving bowl. Add all of the ingredients and mix well. Adjust the seasoning, to taste. Refrigerate for 30 minutes and serve with lemon wedges.

MUSSELS WITH GARLIC AND WHITE WINE

Ingredients

2 lbs. mussels, cleaned

Extra virgin olive oil

2 large shallots, finely chopped

3 garlic cloves, chopped

1 cup dry white wine, pinot grigio

Kosher salt, to taste

Red pepper flakes, to taste

2 tbsp. flat-leaf parsley, chopped

2 tbsp. fresh basil, chopped

2 tbsp. unsalted butter, cubed

Directions

Rinse and scrub the mussels under cold water. Coat the bottom of a medium stock pot with extra virgin olive oil. Add the garlic and shallots and sauté over medium heat until translucent and aromatic, about 5 minutes.

Add the white wine, kosher salt and red pepper flakes and heat through. Raise heat to high, add the mussels, cover and cook until all of the mussels are open, about 5 minutes. Discard any shells that do not open.

Add the parsley, basil, butter and stir together. Remove from the heat. Transfer to a large serving bowl. Serve immediately with crusty bread.

AUNT FANNY'S STUFFED CALAMARI

Ingredients

10 medium calamari tubes, cleaned

3 cups seasoned breadcrumbs

5 cloves of garlic, minced

1/4 cup flat-leaf parsley, chopped

Extra virgin olive oil

1/2 lb. lump crab meat, cleaned

5 shallots, diced

Kosher salt, to taste

Coarse black pepper, to taste

10 fresh basil leaves

32 oz. can whole plum tomatoes (Scalfani® is my preference)

10 round toothpicks

Directions

Preheat oven to 350°F. Wash and clean calamari. Lay the tubes on paper towels to remove all moisture completely.

Heat 2 tbsp. olive oil in a pan over medium heat and sauté shallots until slightly golden brown. Set aside to cool.

In a large bowl, add the bread crumbs, crabmeat, garlic and parsley. Add the cooled sautéed shallots to the mixture. Add kosher salt and pepper, to taste. Toss lightly. If mixture is too dry, add more extra virgin olive oil until the mixture is slightly moist and crumbly.

Stuff each tube, generously but avoid overstuffing, which will cause the tubes to burst during the cooking process. Leave enough room at the opening to thread a toothpick through to hold the tubes closed.

Fry each calamari in a pan with extra virgin olive oil until slightly golden brown. Be careful to not over heat oil. Place calamari in an oven proof deep dish. Squeeze the whole tomatoes with your hands over the top and add half of the tomato juice from the can. Add basil leaves. Season with salt and pepper, to taste. Bake for 25 - 30 minutes. Serve immediately.

DEBORAH'S CRAB CAKES WITH RED PEPPER AIOLI

Ingredients

1 lb. lump crab meat, cleaned

2 shallots, finely diced

1 red bell pepper, roasted and diced

1 large egg, beaten

Kosher salt, to taste

Coarse black pepper, to taste

1/4 cup flat-leaf parsley, chopped

1 1/2 cups panko breadcrumbs

2 garlic cloves, finely minced

2 tsp. Dijon mustard

1/4 fresh cilantro, chopped

Extra virgin olive oil

Directions

Preheat oven to 400°F. Prepare large baking sheet by lining with parchment paper. Brush lightly with extra virgin olive oil and set aside.

Roast the red bell pepper until all sides are blackened, approx. 20 - 30 minutes. Remove from the oven and place the pepper in a small bowl, and cover with plastic wrap until it is cool enough to handle. Remove the blackened outer skin of the pepper, remove the veins and seeds. Dice the red pepper and set aside in a large bowl. Reduce the oven temperature to 350°F.

In a small sauté pan, heat 1 tbsp. of the extra virgin olive oil, add the shallots and garlic. Cook the shallots until they are slightly caramelized and translucent. Once cooled, add both to the bowl with the diced red pepper.

In a separate bowl, beat the egg and add the beaten egg to the bowl with the shallots, garlic and roasted red bell pepper. Add the Dijon mustard, kosher salt and pepper, to taste. Mix together. Add the panko bread crumbs, parsley, cilantro and cleaned lump crab meat. Gently mix together. Add extra virgin olive oil, as needed, to moisten the panko breadcrumbs to the consistency that will hold it together.

To form the crab cakes, fill a 1/4 measuring cup with crab meat mixture. Gently press mixture into measuring cup to form a mold and turn it out gently onto prepared baking sheet.

Drizzle the top of each crab cake, lightly, with extra virgin olive oil. Bake in oven for 20 - 25 minutes until they are a nice golden brown. Serve immediately with lemon wedges and top each crab cake with the red pepper aioli or serve on the side.

ROASTED RED PEPPER AIOLI

Ingredients

1 large red bell pepper, roasted	3 large cloves garlic, do not peel
1/3 cup mayonnaise	1 tsp. capers, rough chopped
1 tbsp. lemon juice	2 tbsp. extra virgin olive oil
1/2 tsp. kosher salt	Pinch coarse black pepper

Directions

Preheat oven to 400°F. Roast the pepper until all sides are blackened. Place the unpeeled garlic cloves in a pan and roast, without pressing, until they are browned on all sides. Remove garlic and set aside.

Place the red pepper in a small bowl and cover with plastic wrap until cool enough to handle. Remove the blackened outer skin of the pepper, remove the veins and seeds. Peel the roasted garlic.

In a food processor or blender, puree the red bell pepper and garlic until smooth. Blend in the mayonnaise. With the machine running, add the olive oil in a slow stream. Add the capers, lemon juice, salt and pepper, to taste and pulse until just combined. Serve on the side with crab cakes or on top of each crab cake.

ZUPPA DI PESCE

Ingredients

3 lbs. calamari, cleaned and cut into bite size pieces

2 dozen little neck clams, cleaned

2 lbs. mussels, cleaned

32 jumbo shrimp, cleaned and deveined

6 garlic cloves, finely minced

2 tbsp. flat-leaf parsley, chopped

3 tbsp. fresh basil, chopped

Extra virgin olive oil

Red pepper flakes, to taste

Kosher salt, to taste

Dry white wine, splash

3 (35 oz. can) Scalfani Italian Whole Peeled Tomatoes®

Directions

Cover the bottom of a large stock pot with extra virgin olive oil and brown the garlic, slightly. Pulse tomatoes for a 5 second count in a blender and add to the pot. Season lightly with salt and red pepper flakes, to taste. Bring to a low boil and reduce heat. Add a splash of white wine, parsley, basil and simmer for 20 minutes.

Add the cleaned calamari and simmer for 30 - 40 minutes, stirring often. Add the shrimp and simmer for 5 - 8 minutes. Add the clams and mussels. Simmer for an additional 10 minutes, until all the clams and mussels are open. Discard any mussels or clams that do not open.

Serve over linguine topped with fresh chopped parsley or with crusty bread.

DEBORAH'S BAKED CLAMS

Ingredients

3 dozen little neck clams, opened, chopped and clean shells

3 tbsp. flat-leaf parsley, chopped

2 cups seasoned breadcrumbs

3 - 4 tbsp. extra virgin olive oil

3 garlic cloves, finely chopped

Kosher salt, to taste

Coarse black pepper, to taste

1/3 cup chicken broth

Directions

Preheat oven to 450°F. In a bowl, combine the bread crumbs, garlic, parsley, chopped clams, kosher salt and pepper, to taste. Add the extra virgin olive oil and stir until combined. Add chicken broth until the mixture is crumbly and moist. Taste to check the seasoning, add more salt and pepper, if needed.

Add the mixture to each clam shell and place on a sheet tray. Add a little water to the pan to keep the clams moist. Drizzle the top of each clam with extra virgin olive oil. Place the tray in the oven and bake for 20 minutes until the bread crumbs are a nice golden brown and crispy.

Transfer to a platter and serve, immediately, with lemon wedges.

COCONUT SHRIMP WITH MANGO CHUTNEY

Ingredients

Canola oil, for frying

1/2 tsp. kosher salt

1 cup shredded coconut

24 jumbo shrimp, peeled, cleaned and deveined

1/2 cup plain bread crumbs

2 pinches ground cayenne pepper

2 egg whites

Directions

Season bread crumbs with salt, and cayenne pepper. In a bowl, combine the coconut and seasoned bread crumbs together. In a separate bowl, slightly beat the egg whites. Dip the shrimp into the egg whites, then coat with the coconut breading. Heat enough oil for frying over medium heat. Fry the shrimp for 5 minutes or until evenly golden and crispy.

MANGO CHUTNEY

Ingredients

3 firm-ripe mangoes, peeled and diced

1/2 cup red bell pepper, chopped

1 green chile, seeded and sliced

1 lime, juiced

1/4 cup extra virgin olive oil

2 garlic cloves

1/2 cup red onion, chopped

1 tbsp. green onion, chopped

1/2 cup cilantro leaves

Kosher salt, to taste

Directions

With the exception of the extra virgin olive oil and salt add all of the ingredients to the food processor or blender. While blending, slowly add the extra virgin olive oil and blend until thick and smooth. Add salt, to taste. Serve with the coconut shrimp, as a dipping sauce.

LASAGNA…AN ITALIAN LOVE STORY

Lasagna has been one of my all-time favorite Italian dish, for as far back as I can remember, and in my research of this rich, and flavorful Italian classic, believe it or not, it comes with a history lesson. There are a few theories, but here's the Italian one…Lasagna originated in Italy, in the region of Emilia-Romagna. Traditional lasagna is made by layering pasta with layers of sauce, made with a ragù or a béchamel, and Parmagiano Reggiano. In other regions, it is common to find lasagna made with ricotta or mozzarella cheese, tomato sauce, various meats (ground beef, pork or chicken), a variation of vegetables (spinach, zucchini, and mushrooms), and typically flavored with wine, garlic, onion, and oregano. In all cases, the lasagna is baked in the oven.

Lasagne calde, calde le lasagne, caldeee! History states that forty years ago, you could hear vendors bellow those words from the busy platform of the Bologna railway station. Though lasagna vendors don't exist today, **Lasagna alla Bolognese** remains the most famous recipe in Italy, and throughout Europe. In Italy, there are countless regional variations of lasagna. Ingredients differ according to place and local custom, but the distinctive character of lasagna remains the same…layers of flat or curly noodles, separated by layers of rich gravy or sauces, a focus ingredient like meat, fish or vegetables, all baked up into one glorious masterpiece of flavor. While lasagna was born in Italy, a familiar hot slice of this cheesy, rich comfort food makes it one of the most commonly craved Italian dishes in homes, and restaurants all around the world.

As a child, I was totally addicted to lasagna, and it was a regular dish served on Christmas Day, and as a special birthday dinner. In between those special occasions, as an adult, it was always my main entrée selection at specific Italian restaurants that I knew made an outstanding version of this Italian classic. And in my opinion, there were very few restaurants who could accomplish this feat.

My first introduction to learning how to prepare, and master an outstanding lasagna was by watching my Aunt Fanny, who besides my father, was one of the first great influences in my life with perfecting my cooking skills. Staying true to our Napolitano decent, her **Lasagna Napoletana** included layers of curly lasagna noodles, gravy (yes, *gravy* not sauce), ricotta cheese, mozzarella, grated cheese, and these tiny meatballs, which were the size of a marble. As tedious as it was to make those tiny meatballs, Aunt Fanny never faltered from putting every ounce of love, and perfection into her lasagna. And as a child, to a teenager to a young adult to a grown up, you couldn't wait to cut into Aunt Fanny's lasagna to find those delicious tiny meatballs.

A Sunday morning lesson at Aunt Fanny's always included her masterpiece of a Sunday gravy. Her gravy, more often than not, always included meatballs, Italian sausage, pork, **braciole pelle di maiale** (pig skin braciole), and beef **braciole.** This is similar to what mine is today, with a bit of a variation, and absolutely, no *braciole pelle di maiale*...only because my children and grandchildren won't eat it, and it's not at the top of the health conscious favorite food list.

Another great cooking influence in my life is my mother-in-law, Angela, fondly known as Nanny Angie. Honestly, she is, by far, the most talented cook I know. I have watched this woman for over 40 years, turn out exceptional and delicious food in the smallest to the largest of kitchens. Her food and presentation make your mouth salivate as you watch her cook. Your mouth hums with absolute pleasure while eating her food. You always walk away from her table feeling completely intoxicated from the experience, and with a *belly* so full and satisfied.

If I learned anything from Nanny Angie, it was that cooking is about pleasing people, a lot of love and passion were musts, and it will always come through in your food. Presentation is crucial, and sitting back, watching people eat your food with complete and utter enjoyment would be your reward. She taught me cooking is a labor of love, which took planning, creativity, patience, and precision. Amongst her many masterpiece dishes, her lasagna is right at the top of my all-time favorites.

For Nanny Angie, lasagna wasn't a regular everyday dish, it was saved for holidays, and special occasions. Her lasagna wasn't much different than Aunt Fanny's, with the exception that hers did not include any meat. Exact precision went into the amount of ricotta cheese, mozzarella, and grated cheese that was used in her lasagna. You can easily overdo it with the cheese, which would create a runny, cheesy mess on your plate but not Nanny Angie's...it was perfect every time. Her lasagna took time, patience, and she was meticulous with each layer.

It's hard to describe what it was like watching her make this masterpiece, and the only words that come to mind...it was an *artistic creation* being prepared right before your eyes. There was a rhythm, a glow, and a sense of pride surrounding her with everything she cooked. Cooking is truly an art, you have to love it, and have a complete passion for cooking to turn out mouthwatering, and tasteful delicacies, such as *Nanny Angie's Lasagna*.

Passing on family traditions is so important to me, and I must admit, with great pride, over the years, my daughter, Jennifer must have been paying attention to the preparation, and skills that went into making a lasagna because she too has mastered the art of making a perfect dish of lasagna. My only hope is that she continues to pay attention, and for as long as I am able, I will continue to teach my granddaughters, too. For me, cooking together in the kitchen, and sharing family recipes, along with secrets passed from one generation to the next is what family is all about.

One of the positive side effects from the labor of making the meatballs, frying the gravy meat, stirring the gravy, and layering the intoxicating goodness of the lasagna noodles, the cheeses, and the gravy on top of each other is the guaranteed knowledge of knowing...there will always be leftovers.

As I have stated many times, it's extremely hard for me to recite or write my recipes down on paper. I learned from the best of the best, and exact measurements were rarely used. I can do all of the recipes by osmosis but in the spirit of giving back, I have done my best to capture all of the steps, and I hope you enjoy all of them.

Lastly, when in the kitchen, always remember Julia Childs words, *"Cooking is one failure after another, and that's how you finally learn...no one is born a great cook, one learns by doing."*

Buon appetito!

NANNY ANGIE'S LASAGNA

Ingredients

5 cups gravy (Nana's Gravy - Sunday Pot of Love, recipe to follow)

32 oz. whole milk ricotta   1/4 cup flat-leaf parsley, chopped

1 cup Pecorino Romano cheese, grated

2 large eggs

1 box lasagna (15 sheets, cooked al dente) *see note below

4 1/2 cups mozzarella cheese, shredded

Coarse black pepper, to taste

Directions

Preheat oven to 350°F. Combine ricotta, 3/4 cup grated cheese, and parsley in a bowl. Season, to taste, black pepper. Add the eggs and mix all together.

Spread 1/2 cup gravy over bottom of 13 by 9 inch baking dish. Place 5 lasagna sheets over gravy, overlapping to fit. Spread half of the ricotta mixture evenly over the sheets. Sprinkle 2 cups of mozzarella cheese evenly over ricotta mixture. Then, spoon 1 1/2 cups of gravy over cheese, spreading with spatula to cover. Repeat layering with 5 additional lasagna sheets, ricotta mixture, 2 cups mozzarella and 1 1/2 cups gravy. Top with the last 5 lasagna sheets with gravy, 1/2 cup of mozzarella, and 1/4 cup grated cheese.

Cover the baking dish with aluminum foil, and bake for about 40 - 45 minutes. Uncover, then bake until hot, and bubbly, about 20 minutes. Let the lasagna stand for 15 minutes before serving.

Note: A quick option is to use the No Boil lasagna sheets, which also produces a perfect lasagna, and saves a lot of time.

NANA'S SUNDAY POT OF LOVE

Since I was a little girl, Sunday's have always had a special meaning. When you're fortunate enough to grow up in a multi-cultural family, like myself, you are born into a world of some magnificent foods, and family traditions that stay with you for a lifetime. My only wish has always been to pass on those childhood memories, traditions, recipes, and for them to be replicated for generations to come. In this chapter, I will take you on a journey on how I got to a place that I call…"***Nana's Sunday Pot of Love.***"

My dad was born and raised in Puerto Rico. He came to New York at the age of 16. My mother was born in Harlem, and her parents, (my grandparents) were Italian immigrants from Sarno, Italy, which is just outside of Naples. They eventually settled in Mt. Vernon, New York. Me, an American, born and raised into a family of Puerto Rican and Napolitano descent…I call it, *"the best of both worlds."* I feel cheated in a sense that I wasn't fortunate enough to grow up with grandparents. My maternal grandparents passed on when I was very young, and I only have small bits, and pieces of a memory of my grandmother, who left us when I was 6 years old.

My paternal grandparents lived in Puerto Rico, and my grandfather would never get on a plane to come to New York, to visit or anywhere else, for that matter…his famous words were, ***"If God meant for me to fly, he would have made me a bird."*** I did have the opportunity to visit them, twice in their lifetime, but that's a story for another day.

While Puerto Rican and Italian food cultures are completely different, family bonds, and family meals were extremely important, and strong in both cultures. Interestingly enough, my father was a better cook than my mother, but we could never tell her this…she would have been crushed. My dad was the first influence in my life, where I learned to be completely passionate about food, and the art of cooking. His belief with cooking…***"cooking took time and you just couldn't rush it."***

First, let me start with my Puerto Rican heritage. I have memories of waking up, on Saturday mornings, to my dad just coming back from the Bronx (I always regretted not asking where, exactly), with this fabulous Spanish bread, ***Pan de Agua*** (Puerto Rican Water Bread), which was always still warm, and the butter would just melt right into it. Heavenly!

There was always that little white box that contained **Budín** (Puerto Rican Bread Pudding). It was so delicious, and while it is impossible for me to describe its flavor, and taste, I can tell you this, I have never found a replication of it that can come even close to it. I have searched, and searched, and that flavor, smell, and taste are burned into my childhood memory, and I am remain hopeful that one day we will meet again.

Some Puerto Rican dishes that were pretty much a staple in our house...*pernil* (Puerto Rican slow roasted pork), **arroz con gandules** (rice with pigeon peas), **arroz con pollo** (chicken and rice), **tostones** (fried green plantains), and flan that delicious vanilla custard, with just a touch of a caramel flavor.

However, there are three dishes that hold the fondest memories for me, from my childhood until today. *Paella* was a special treat, and my dad would take us to a restaurant in City Island (again, regrettably, I don't remember the name). The length of time it takes to make this one pot meal, which includes chicken, chorizo, mussels, clams, shrimp, pork, and some other great ingredients, and flavors is well worth the wait.

Then there were *pasteles*, which in the Puerto Rican culture are a cherished culinary recipe, and they are typically made only around the holidays (most often, Christmas). Pasteles are a soft dough-like masa wrapped in a banana or plantain leaf and boiled. In the center of the dough there can be variations of choice pieces of chopped meat, shellfish, chicken, raisins, spices, capers, olives, sofrito and garbanzo beans. Puerto Rican pasteles are similar in shape, size, and cooking technique to tamales. I don't have the knowledge or the experience with making them to give them the justice they so rightfully deserve. What I do know, is they are extremely labor intensive. They are made in batches of a hundred or more, and when you receive these culinary treasures as a gift, sharing is something you really think about, and more often than not, you don't want to part with them. With the help of my great-niece, Stefanie, we put together a pastele recipe for those of you who might be adventurous or interested in taking a stab at making a batch.

I have come across many people who have asked, *what is sofrito?* Simply put, sofrito is an aromatic blend of herbs and spices used throughout the Caribbean, especially Puerto Rico. It's used to season countless dishes, which include stews, beans, rice, and meats. In most cases, it is the base, which the rest of the recipe is built upon. Sofrito blends range in color from green to orange to red. It also has a range in taste from mild to pungent to spicy. Contributing flavors and ingredients include cilantro and **ajies dulces** (sweet chili peppers).

Lastly, I think the meal cooked by my father that we still talk about until this day with my sisters, children and nephew is his **Bistec Encebollado**, which is fondly known as Poppy's Steak & Onions. It is strips of beef medallions, pounded thinly, and sliced onions, which were marinated together for hours in garlic, oregano, olive oil, vinegar, and Poppy's secret sofrito, and adobo. He would sauté everything, and stew all of it together, and then it was served with white rice and beans.

While it may not sound like much, trust me, after the bread dipping into the juices, and the fighting for the last piece of succulent steak, everyone left that meal extremely satisfied. This was just one of many dishes that I wished I paid closer attention to. Even though we all know the ingredients or we think we do, no one has perfected it nor has anyone come close to replicating *Poppy's Steak and Onions.*

Typically, they say your mother's heritage, and traditions dominate your upbringing. For me, while my father had a great family influence in my life, he had very little of his own family in New York, and with my mother being one of eight children (4 sisters and 4 brothers), it was her Italian side that dominated my upbringing. Our home was fairly small, and most Sunday dinners were spent with one of my relatives on my mother's side but that's not to say there weren't meals at my mother's table. She always found room, and there was always enough.

Growing up in a large Italian family, (4 generations of 90 or more, and growing), there is such a wealth of traditions, and knowledge around cooking. I learned from many, if not, from all of my aunts, who I consider to be some of the best Italian home cooks, how to perfect my cooking skills, and the precision, along with the finesse in presenting food. They truly cooked with love, a lot of passion, and for each one of them, it was always about pleasing those sitting at their table, and the gratification they received from your enjoyment of their food.

Through the years, I have stood and watched many of my aunts, at their stoves, mentally absorbing their skills and techniques. With the exception of baking, which is pure science, they were cooks who measured nothing, and they could never really recite a recipe without saying, a pinch, a handful or palm full measurement. Everything was measured visually, and by taste. It's a talent that's hard to learn unless you really enjoy cooking or more importantly, paid attention.

I grew up on Italian favorites such as, *pasta fagioli* (macaroni and beans), *bistecca alla pizzaiola* (steak, marinara, garlic, oregano, mushrooms, onions, and stewed in one pot), and *pasta e piselli con carne macinata* – sautéed onions, and garlic with ground beef, add peas, penne, small elbow macaroni or ditalini, and meld everything together. Serve it with some grated cheese, and crushed red pepper flakes…*ahhh, a feast!*

One of my lasting memories of my Aunt Dotty is her famous, ***patate e uova frittata*** (potato and egg omelet), which included five pounds of potatoes, and at least a dozen or more eggs. She would cook the potatoes in this old cast iron pan, which the family still has today, and when the potatoes were nearly done, she added the beaten eggs. Once the frittata was done, it was about 3 inches high, and the potatoes always had a crisp to them. Visually, it is an absolute work of art, and since the pan is so heavy, my Uncle Marty was in charge of turning it over so that it can continue to cook, and once done, onto a serving dish and he would carefully place the masterpiece on the table.

Sunday's were always about family visits, eating, and playing with your cousins, who lived near, or far. It could be any one of your relatives house that you would visit...traveling to the Bronx or to Flushing or to Brooklyn or to somewhere in between. Whoever's house it was, it was almost a guarantee the smell of meatballs frying would immediately hit your senses once you walked through the front door, and that Sunday pot of gravy would be simmering on the stove. The Sunday meal was considered a feast, and that pot of gravy always included meatballs, pork, braciole, and ***pelle di maiale*** (pig skin), which again, while today it is considered so unhealthy, back then it was so delicious, and it just melted in your mouth after being cooked for hours in the gravy.

Before we ventured out to visit family, my dad always took a ride, after Sunday mass, to the Italian deli, Zuccarelli's, on Gramatan Ave, and to Dante's Italian Bakery on 241st Street in the Bronx. It was a given, you never visited family without bringing pastries. I can remember walking into that deli, and even as a child, you were immediately intoxicated by the aroma of the delicacies on display. The Italian cold cuts, specialties, and breads that were purchased were either for the week's lunches or for a snack, if you were still hungry when you arrived home from the Sunday family dinner, which typically started at 2pm.

And as for the Italian pastries, who could resist a *cannoli* or a *chocolate éclair* or a *sfogliatelle* or a *pasticiotto*…just to name a few.

All of these influences have added to my current day traditional Italian Sunday dinners, and holiday's with my family. Sadly, my parents are no longer with us, but the traditions they instilled in me live on. When my children were growing up, my son would smell those Sunday morning meatballs in his sleep, and he would immediately wake up to eat a few of them that were just fried, and right before they went into the pot of gravy. As he got older, and those teenage years rolled around, he didn't get up as easily but I always made sure there was a small bowl of fried meatballs left on the kitchen counter for him.

Before becoming a Nana, my dream had always been for my grandchildren to wake up on a Sunday morning, and say, *"I want to go to Nana's to eat her meatballs."* Today, with the busy lives that many people lead, and with both parents in the workplace, along with keeping up with children's sports activities, school work, social events, just to name a few, Sunday dinners, as I grew up knowing them to be, has changed. However, for me, I remain true to my upbringing, and family traditions. A Sunday dinner, the holiday's or any meal, for that matter, will never be anything less than it was for me growing up…not for this Nana.

Today, my sisters, and I have grown our immediate family into seventeen, which now includes our own children, grandchildren, nieces and nephews to great nieces and nephews. Most Sunday's, my table is filled with family, and whoever shows up, shows up. It's a given that there is always enough, there is always room, and an invite is not necessary.

Over the years, the endless compliments I have received have been my biggest gratification. My 4-year old nephew, Vincent says, *"Aunt Deb's meatballs are the best"* and he very rarely will he eat anyone's meatballs, but mine. With every Christmas Eve, in the past, that was hosted at another family members house, it was a given that I would receive a frantic call from my son and nephew confirming I was still doing the cooking, and lastly, my cooking being referred to as *"gourmet"* by my nephew's wife, Monica is the ultimate compliment I could ever receive.

I always tell my daughter, and now I include my daughter-in-law, and granddaughter's…pay attention because I am not going to be around forever (reality) but for as long as I am here and I am physically able, Nana's stove will always have a *Sunday Pot of Love* simmering on it, and it will always be filled with my famous meatballs, sausage, and succulent pork that falls off the bone.

The meal will always begin with antipasto, which typically includes fresh mozzarella, fried sweet and hot peppers, an assortment of Italian olives, and soppressata.

There will always be fresh Italian bread or a homemade focaccia, along with one of my famous dessert creations. Dessert can be anything from a puffed pastry apple tart served warm with homemade French vanilla ice cream to chocolate lava cake to zeppoles with apricot dipping sauce.

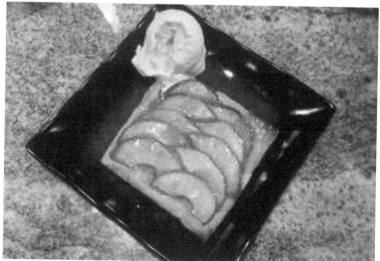

Cooking together as a family builds strong family bonds, memories, and it brings everyone together for laughter, sharing old and new stories, learning, and teaching old family traditions. So surround yourself with family, pour a cup of coffee or espresso or a glass of wine...break out the flour, and dust off that mixer, chop some garlic, and take out the hidden cast iron or frying pan. Get yourself some extra virgin olive oil, and some great Italian cheeses, olives, bread, and put on your *mad scientist hat*!

When you're passionate about food, the possibilities are endless. In the end there will always be a tasteful surprise, and more importantly, it's a feast with the people you love…family. The family this Nana loves, will always have a place at her stove, and her table, and unconditionally, they will always hold a special place in her heart, and in her life, along with *"Nana's Sunday Pot of Love."*

La famiglia e mangiare!

PERNIL - ROAST PORK SHOULDER

Ingredients

8 - 9 lb. bone-in, skin-on pork shoulder

3 tbsp. extra virgin olive oil

1 tbsp. coarse black pepper

Bunch of fresh oregano

4 cloves garlic, finely chopped

2 tbsp. kosher salt

2 tsp. adobo seasoning

2 tbsp. white wine vinegar

Directions

Place the pork, fat-side up, in a roasting pan and using a sharp knife, score the surface of the meat with small slits. Mash the garlic, oregano, adobo, salt, and pepper into a paste. Place the paste in a bowl and stir in the extra virgin oil and vinegar. Rub the garlic paste all over the pork and into the slits. Cover the pork with plastic wrap and marinate in the refrigerator for at least 3 hours or overnight.

Allow the meat to sit at room temperature for 1 hour before cooking. Preheat oven to 350°F degrees. Cover the pork tightly with aluminum foil. Roast the covered pork, until fork tender and internal temperature reads 145°F, for 3 to 3 1/2 hours. Increase the oven to 450°F. Cook pork, uncovered, until the skin is brown and crisp, 20 - 35 minutes. Check the pan every 10 minutes and add 1/4 cup of water, at a time, if the pan becomes dry.

Let the meat rest on a cutting board for 10 minutes before slicing.

ARROZ CON GANDULES
RICE WITH PIGEON PEAS

Ingredients

1 tbsp. extra virgin olive oil

2 cups long grain rice

1 packet GOYA® Sazón

15 oz. can pigeon peas (drained and rinsed)

1/2 cup sofrito (combination of chopped onions, red bell pepper, garlic, cilantro and tomatoes)

1/2 cup chopped country ham

4 cups water

Directions

Heat extra virgin olive oil in a 6-quart pot. Sauté all of the sofrito ingredients and chopped ham for 1 minute. Add the rice, water, sazón and gandules.

Bring to a boil. Let boil for 2 to 3 minutes. Cover, reduce the heat to medium low and cook for 35 to 40 minutes. When finished cooking, stir the rice before serving. It should be light and fluffy.

ARROZ CON POLLO - CHICKEN AND RICE

Ingredients

1 tbsp. extra virgin olive oil

4 chicken thighs

4 chicken drumsticks

2 tsp. kosher salt

1/2 tsp. coarse black pepper

1 small onion, chopped

2 cloves garlic, minced

1 red bell pepper, chopped

1 tsp. ground cumin

1 bunch cilantro, chopped

1 green bell pepper, chopped

1 tbsp. tomato paste

1 3/4 cups canned tomatoes, drained and chopped

2 cups low-sodium chicken broth

1 cup long-grain rice

2 tbsp. flat-leaf parsley, chopped

Directions

In a large, deep pot, heat the oil over moderately high heat. Season the chicken with 1/4 tsp. each of the salt and pepper. Cook the chicken, turning, until well browned on all sides, about 8 minutes. Remove the chicken from the pot and pour off excess fat, with the exception of 2 tbsp.

Reduce the heat to low-medium. Add the ham, onion and garlic and cook until the onion become translucent, about 2 minutes. Add the red and green bell peppers and cook, stirring occasionally, until the peppers start to soften, about 3 minutes.

Add the tomatoes, tomato paste, cumin, cilantro, broth, and the remaining 1 3/4 tsp. salt, 1/4 tsp. pepper and bring to a simmer. Stir in the rice and add the chicken. Simmer, partially covered, over low heat until the chicken and rice are just done, 20 to 25 minutes. Sprinkle with parsley before serving.

TOSTONES DE PLATANO VERDE
FRIED GREEN PLANTAINS

Ingredients

4 green plantains

Kosher salt, to taste

Canola oil, for frying

Directions

Peel the plantains and cut into 1-inch pieces. Heat enough oil for frying in a large frying pan. Without overcrowding pan, fry the plantains in batches for 2 - 3 minutes per side. Drain on a paper towels.

Flatten each plantain by using a tostonera or the bottom of a heavy can to about 1/4 inch thickness. In a bowl of warm salted water, dip each fried plantain one at a time and drain well on paper towels. Reheat the pan with oil and add additional oil, if needed. Fry each plantain again for about one minute or until golden brown. Drain on paper towels and sprinkle with a little salt. Serve immediately or top with Garlic Mojo (recipe to follow)

GARLIC MOJO

Ingredients

3 garlic cloves, minced

1/4 cup extra virgin olive oil

1/2 tsp. kosher salt

1 tbsp. fresh lime juice

2 tbsp. fresh orange juice

Pinch of coarse black pepper

Directions

In a small bowl, whisk all ingredients together. Top each plantain with a little mojo and serve on the side.

FLAN

Ingredients

1 3/4 cups whipping cream

1 cup whole milk

Pinch of salt

1 vanilla bean, split lengthwise

3 large eggs

2 large yolks

7 tbsp. sugar

Directions

Position rack in the center of oven and preheat to 350°F. Combine cream, milk and salt in a heavy medium saucepan. Scrape seeds from vanilla bean into cream mixture and add bean pod. Bring to a simmer over medium heat. Remove from heat and let cream mixture stand 30 minutes. While the mixture is setting, cook the caramel sauce. Prepare six 3/4 cup ramekins.

Whisk the eggs, egg yolks and 7 tbsp. sugar in a medium bowl just until blended. Gradually and gently whisk cream mixture into egg mixture without creating lots of foam. Pour custard through a small sieve into prepared ramekins, dividing evenly (mixture will fill ramekins). Pour enough hot water into baking pan to come halfway up the sides of the ramekins.

Bake until the center of each ramekin is gently set, about 40 minutes. Transfer to rack and cool. Cover and chill about 2 hours or overnight.

CARAMEL

Ingredients

1 cup sugar

1/3 cup water

Directions

Combine sugar and water in a heavy medium saucepan. Stir over low heat until sugar dissolves. Increase heat to high and cook without stirring until syrup turns a deep amber. Brush down sides of pan with a wet pastry brush and swirl the pan occasionally, about 10 minutes. Pour into ramekins.

PAELLA

Ingredients

1 cup water

1 tsp. saffron threads

6 cups low-sodium chicken broth

4 boneless chicken thighs, halved

1 tsp. sweet paprika

1 tsp. dried oregano

Kosher salt, to taste

Coarse black pepper, to taste

1 tbsp. extra virgin olive oil

1/2 lb. chorizo sausage, cut thick

1 dozen little neck clams, cleaned

1 Spanish onion, finely chopped

1 cup red bell pepper, chopped

1 cup canned diced tomatoes

3 garlic cloves, minced

3 cups Arborio or short grain rice

1 cup frozen sweet peas

8 mussels, scrubbed and cleaned

1 lb. jumbo shrimp, cleaned

Bunch of flat-leaf parsley, chopped

1/4 cup fresh lemon juice

Lemon wedges, optional

Directions

Remove skin from the chicken and season with kosher salt, pepper, sweet paprika and oregano. Marinate in the refrigerator for 1 hour.

Combine water, saffron, and broth in a large stock pot. Bring to a simmer. Keep warm over low heat.

Peel and devein the shrimp, leaving tails intact and set aside.

Heat extra virgin olive oil in a large, wide and shallow pan over medium-high heat. Add the chicken and sauté for 2 - 3 minutes on each side. Remove from the pan. Add the chorizo and sauté for 2 minutes. Remove from pan. Reduce heat to medium. Add the onions, garlic, parsley, red bell pepper and sauté for 5 minutes. Add the diced tomatoes and cook for 5 minutes.

Add the rice and sauté for 1 minute, stirring constantly. Add the broth mixture, chicken and sausage. Bring to a low boil and cook for 10 minutes, stirring frequently and gently so the rice cooks evenly and absorbs the liquid.

Add the mussels and clams to the pan, nestling them into rice. Cook for 5 minutes or until shells open. Discard any unopened shells. Arrange shrimp, heads down into the rice mixture and cook for 8 minutes. Add the peas, sprinkle with 1/4 cup lemon juice and parsley. Remove from the heat, cover and let stand 10 minutes. Serve with lemon wedges, if desired.

PASTELES

Courtesy of my great-niece, Stefanie

Ingredients for Stuffing

2 lbs. diced pork

1 small onion, chopped

4 cloves garlic, finely chopped

1 tsp. dried oregano

1/2 cup green olives with pimento, chopped

6 oz. can pimentos, chopped

4 ajíces dulces (small sweet peppers)

2 tbsp. GOYA® recaito

1 tbsp. GOYA® adobo

1/2 can garbanzo beans, rinsed

Extra virgin olive oil

Directions

Coat the bottom of a large pan with extra virgin olive oil. Brown the pork pieces in a pan. Add all of the remaining ingredients. Cook on low heat for approx. 30 minutes, until the pork is cooked all the way through. Set aside and let cool.

Ingredients for Masa Dough

4 lbs. yautía

1 tbsp. kosher salt

2 tbsp. milk

6 green plantains

Achiote oil

Directions

In a large bowl, peel and grate the yautía and the green plantains together. Add salt, milk and enough achiote oil to moisten the dough and add a little color. **Note:** For easier handling, make the masa one day in advance.

Ingredients for Wrapping

40 banana leaves (cut into approx. 10 inch square)

20 pieces of parchment paper (cut into approx. 8 inch squares)

20 pieces of kitchen string (each 20 inches long)

Directions

Cut a piece of parchment paper about 10 inch square. Cut two pieces of banana leaf about 8 inch squares. Lay the parchment paper on a flat work surface. Place one cut banana leaf in the center of the parchment paper.

Brush a few drops of achiote oil onto the center of the banana leaf. Place about 2 spoonful's of masa onto the oil in the center of the banana leaf. Flatten and spread out the dough evenly, but do not go over the edge of the leaf. Place 1 spoonful of the meat filling in the center of the masa.

Place another 2 spoonful's of the masa on top of the meat filling. Spread the masa evenly to cover the filling. Brush a few drops of achiote oil on one side of the second piece of banana leaf. Place the leaf, oiled side down, on top of the masa.

Bring the top edge and bottom edge of the parchment paper up so that the edges meet evenly over the top of the pastele. Fold down the edges, forming a horizontal seam. Fold up the ends of the parchment paper and flip the wrapped pastele over.

Tie the pastel with string to hold it together. The string should run of lengthwise and twice across the width. This will hold the pasteles securely together during the cooking process.

Bring a stock pot of salted water to a boil. The water should cover the pasteles. Boil for 1 hour. Untie and serve.

Note: Pasteles can be frozen raw. In place of parchment paper and banana leaves, aluminum foil can be used to wrap the pasteles. Be sure the foil is securely closed.

Suggestion: Make it a pastele party. Gather family and friends. Set up an assembly line. Put on your favorite Latin music, crack open a bottle of wine and assemble the pasteles.

BISTEC ENCEBOLLADO
POPPY'S STEAK AND ONIONS

Ingredients

2 garlic cloves, minced

1 tsp. GOYA® Adobo seasoning

1/4 cup white vinegar

1 cup water

3 large onions, thinly sliced

1 tsp. coarse black pepper

1/4 tsp. dried oregano

2 lbs. beef steak, sliced thin

2 tbsp. canola oil

Directions

Pound beef steak to 1/4 inch thickness. Place all ingredients in a gallon-size plastic bag. Seal the bag. Shake well to mix all of the ingredients together. Refrigerate for at least 4 hours or overnight.

Place contents of bag into a large heavy skillet and bring it to a boil. Lower the heat, cover and cook for 40 minutes or until the meat is very tender. Serve with white rice, pink beans and tostones.

NANA'S GRAVY - SUNDAY POT OF LOVE

Ingredients

1 1/2 lb. Italian sausage (sweet or hot or combination of both)

10 pork spare ribs (small but meaty)   Bunch of fresh basil

1 medium onion, peeled and cut in half

2 (35 oz. can) Scalfani Italian Whole Peeled Tomatoes® (This brand is my preference. I find them to be the most consistent canned tomatoes but feel free to use your favorite.)

3 (28 oz. can) crushed tomatoes   1 (6 oz. can) tomato paste

Kosher salt, to taste   Coarse black pepper, to taste

Extra virgin olive oil (enough for frying)   1/4 cup sugar

Directions

Season both sides of pork spare ribs with salt and pepper. Coat the bottom of 8 quart Dutch oven or heavy pot with enough olive oil to fry. Heat extra virgin olive oil over medium heat. Add pork spare ribs, and fry until there is a nice sear on all sides. Remove from pot, and set aside.

In same pan, brown the Italian sausage until they browned on all sides and cooked halfway through (approx. 15 min). Remove from pot, and set aside.

Add additional oil, if needed. Prepare meatballs (recipe below), and fry meatballs, in batches (do not overcrowd) until cooked all the way through. Add onion, and brown. Drain off excess oil. Do not wash pot. Reduce the heat to low, and add all of the meat (pork, sausage and meatballs) back into the pot.

Pulse whole peeled tomatoes in a blender for a 5 second count, and add to the pot. Add crushed tomatoes and tomato paste. Take one empty can of crushed tomatoes, fill it to the top with water, and transfer back and forth between all cans of tomatoes, including the tomato paste. Add the water to the pot of gravy and stir.

Add a bunch of basil leaves (handful, not chopped). Add the sugar. Season with kosher salt, to taste. Stir and simmer on low heat for approximately 3 hours.

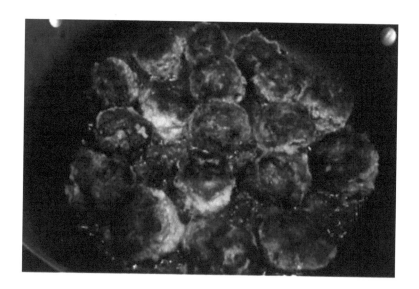

DEBORAH'S MEATBALLS

Ingredients

1 1/2 lb. ground meat (combination of pork, veal and beef)

1 lb. ground beef

2 large eggs

4 cloves garlic, finely minced

Milk (enough to coat bread)

8 large slices of Terranova bread, crust removed and cubed (day old bread)

Kosher salt, to taste

Coarse black pepper, to taste

1/4 cup flat-leaf parsley, chopped

1 cup Pecorino Romano, grated

Directions

Place cubed terranova bread in a large bowl and cover with milk (don't overdo the milk). Let bread soak for approx. 15 min. Squeeze bread and drain off excess milk. Add all of the ground meat, eggs, garlic, parsley, grated cheese, kosher salt and pepper, to taste. Mix together until well incorporated.

To form consistent sized meatballs, use a regular size ice cream scooper. Roll each scoop into a ball and fry until a nice crust is formed on the outside of each meatball. Fry the meatballs in the same pot that you fried the sausage and pork.

Note: The meatball mixture should be a tight consistency, otherwise, the meatballs will fall apart in the gravy, and that's an Italian cook's worst nightmare!

ABOUT THE AUTHOR

Deborah Lugo DeMatteis, Personal Chef, is a native New Yorker, who cooks with love, passion, her heart and soul, and it all comes through in the taste, and presentation of her food. Coming from a large Italian family, and surrounded by inspiration, she learned how to master cooking from those she considers to be some of the best home cooks.

After 33 years of working in the financial industry, Deborah listened to her intuitive inner voice, and has pursued her life passion, and dream. Her vast business knowledge, wisdom, along with her level of confidence, and comfort in the kitchen, and her creative ideas are all possessions she is eagerly willing to share. She works with her clients to ensure their intimate dinner parties, in-home meals, and private or group cooking lessons are what they ultimately envision them to be. Now, in her second cookbook she continues to share some of her Italian and Puerto Rican family traditional holiday recipes, and takes you on the journey of her most cherished memories from her Italian-American and Puerto Rican heritage.

divinedelectables@aol.com
www.divinedelectablesbydeborah.com

Printed in the USA
CPSIA information can be obtained
at www.ICGtesting.com
LVHW061225181223
766700LV00036B/11